Sky

Fly Adventures

Justin Shepherd

Copyright © 2025 *Skylar Shepherd*

All rights reserved.

No part of this book may be reproduced, stored in a retrieval system, or transmitted, in any form or by any means, electronic, mechanical, photocopying, recording, or otherwise, without prior written permission from the publisher, except for brief quotations embodied in critical reviews and certain other noncommercial uses permitted by copyright law.

ISBN: [978-1-80558-381-3]

"Skylar, it's bedtime now,"

Mom called gently from the doorway.

"But Mom, just a few more minutes, please?"

Skylar pleaded, her eyes twinkling with the promise of unsung mischief.

"All right, five more minutes, but then it's straight to bed," Mom surrendered with a soft smile.

Skylar's face lit up.

"Watch this, Mommy!" she yelled, bouncing energetically on her bed.

"Bouncy, bouncy, bouncy!"

"Wow, Skylar, you're almost touching the ceiling! But can you sing a song while you jump?"

Mom challenged, her voice playfully.

Giggling, Skylar began to sing in a melodious voice, "La, la, la, shake your body, shake your body," as she twirled and danced on the mattress.

"And look, Mommy, I've got some cool dance moves too!" Skylar declared, spinning around with her arms spread wide.

Laughing together, Mom reminded, "That was wonderful, but don't forget to brush your teeth, superstar."

"Oops!" Skylar scampered off, her feet thumping softly against the floor. Moments later, the sounds of vigorous brushing filled the air.

"Brush, brush, swish, swish,"

Skylar narrated her actions, making sure her teeth were sparkling clean.

Returning to her room, Skylar threw her arms around Mom.

"You're the best Mommy in the whole world," she said, squeezing tightly.

"And you are my favorite adventurer," Mom replied, hugging her back just as tightly.

As they shared a warm hug, Skylar playfully whispered, "Hey Mommy, before you go... smell my feet!"

Laughing, Mom said playfully.

"Ewww! Feet are not for smelling; they're for walking... and for running into bed!" she tickled Skylar, who giggled and squirmed.

"Good night, Mommy," Skylar yawned, finally feeling the pull of sleep.

"Good night, my little explorer. I can't wait to see what adventures tomorrow brings,"

Mom whispered, turning off the light and closing the door to a soft, dream-filled slumber.